ANNAPOLIS MARYLAND

Annapolis

Travel Guide

2024

Your Ultimate Handbook for Exploring the Sailing Capital of the United States - Discover Historic Landmarks, Cultural Gems, Outdoor Adventures, and Local Cuisine

ROBSON PHILLIP

All rights reserved. No part of this publication may be reproduced, distributed, or transmitted in any form or by any means, including photocopying, recording, or other electronic or mechanical methods, without the prior written permission of the publisher, except in the case of brief quotations embodied in critical reviews and certain other noncommercial uses permitted by copyright law.

Copyright © Robson Phillip, 2024.

Table of Contents

Welcome to Annapolis 8
    Introduction 8
    How to Use This Guide 10

Planning Your Trip 21
    Best Time to Visit 21
    Getting There 23
    Transportation Options 25
    Accommodation Guide 27
    Budgeting Your Trip 29

Historical Overview 33
    Early History 33
    Colonial Annapolis 34
    Annapolis in the 19th and 20th Centuries 36
    Modern-Day Annapolis 38

Top Attractions 42
    United States Naval Academy 42
    Maryland State House 44
    Historic Downtown Annapolis 45
    William Paca House and Garden 47
    Banneker-Douglass Museum 48
    Annapolis Maritime Museum 49
    Summary 51

Cultural Experiences 53
   Local Arts Scene 53
   Museums and Galleries 56
   Theatrical Performances 58
   Annual Events and Festivals 60
Outdoor Activities 64
   Sailing and Boating 65
   Parks and Nature Trails 67
   Water Sports 70
   Golf Courses 71
   Walking Tours 73
Food and Drink 76
   Top Restaurants 77
   Local Cuisine 79
   Craft Breweries 81
   Wineries and Distilleries 82
   Best Coffee Shops 83
Shopping in Annapolis 87
   Historic Downtown Shops 88
   Artisanal Markets 90
   Souvenir Shops 92
   Malls and Boutiques 94
Family-Friendly Activities 97
   Kid-Friendly Attractions 98

Educational Tours 100
Family-Oriented Events 102
Parks and Playgrounds 105
Day Trips and Excursions 108
Chesapeake Bay 109
St. Michaels 110
Baltimore 112
Washington, D.C. 113
Other Nearby Destinations 115
Practical Information 118
Weather and Climate 118
Safety Tips 121
Health and Medical Services 122
Local Customs and Etiquette 123
Emergency Contacts 124
Resources 127
Useful Websites and Apps 127
Local Contacts 131
Conclusion 135
A City Steeped in History 135
Vibrant Cultural Experiences 136
Outdoor Adventures 136
Culinary Delights 137
Family-Friendly Activities 137

Day Trips and Excursions 138

Practical Information 138

A Warm Welcome 139

In Closing 139

Frequently Asked Questions (FAQs) 141

Welcome to Annapolis

Introduction

Nestled on the shores of the Chesapeake Bay, Annapolis is a city that seamlessly blends rich history with vibrant modernity. Known as the "Sailing Capital of the United States," Annapolis offers an enchanting mix of colonial charm, maritime heritage, and a lively cultural scene. This guide is designed to provide you with everything you need to know to make the most of your visit to Annapolis in 2024.

Annapolis is not just the capital of Maryland; it's a city where the past and present collide in the most delightful ways. From the historic streets lined with 18th-century buildings to the bustling waterfront where you can watch sailboats glide by, Annapolis is a place that invites exploration and discovery. Whether you're a history buff, a sailing enthusiast, a foodie, or a family looking for a perfect vacation spot, Annapolis has something to offer you.

As you stroll through the cobblestone streets, you'll find yourself stepping back in time. Historic sites like the Maryland State House and the United States Naval Academy offer a glimpse into the nation's past. Meanwhile, the city's thriving arts scene, diverse culinary offerings, and numerous outdoor activities provide a taste of contemporary Annapolis life.

In this section, we'll introduce you to the city and provide practical information on how to use this guide to plan your trip. So, let's embark on a journey through the heart of Annapolis, a city that promises to captivate and inspire.

How to Use This Guide

To help you navigate your way through Annapolis, this guide is structured into comprehensive sections, each designed to cater to different aspects of your travel experience. Here's a breakdown of what you can expect from each section and how to use this guide effectively:

Planning Your Trip

Start your journey with the "Planning Your Trip" section, which covers the essentials of when to visit, how to get there, and where to stay. This section will help you plan the logistics of your trip, ensuring you have all the necessary information before you arrive.

- **Best Time to Visit**: Discover the ideal seasons to explore Annapolis, taking into account weather, events, and local festivals.

- **Getting There**: Learn about the various transportation options available, including airports, train stations, and major highways.

- **Transportation Options**: Find out the best ways to get around the city, whether by car, public transit, bike, or on foot.

- **Accommodation Guide**: Explore a range of lodging options to suit all budgets and preferences, from luxury hotels to charming bed and breakfasts.

Historical Overview

Dive into the rich history of Annapolis in the "Historical Overview" section. This part of the guide provides a detailed account of the city's past, from its colonial origins to its role in American history.

- **Early History**: Understand the founding and early development of Annapolis.

- **Colonial Annapolis**: Learn about the city's significance during the colonial period and the American Revolution.

- **Annapolis in the 19th and 20th Centuries**: Follow the city's evolution through the Civil War and into the modern era.

- **Modern-Day Annapolis**: Discover how Annapolis has grown and changed in recent years, blending its historical roots with contemporary culture.

Top Attractions

The "Top Attractions" section highlights must-see sights and landmarks that you won't want to miss. This section provides detailed descriptions, visiting tips, and historical context for each location.

- **United States Naval Academy**: Explore the prestigious naval institution and its storied history.

- **Maryland State House**: Visit the oldest state capitol in continuous legislative use.

- **Historic Downtown Annapolis**: Wander through the charming streets and discover colonial architecture, shops, and restaurants.

- **William Paca House and Garden**: Tour the beautifully restored home of a Declaration of Independence signer.

- **Banneker-Douglass Museum**: Delve into Maryland's African American history.

- **Annapolis Maritime Museum**: Learn about the city's maritime heritage and the Chesapeake Bay.

Cultural Experiences

In the "Cultural Experiences" section, immerse yourself in the vibrant arts and cultural scene of Annapolis. This section covers everything from local galleries and museums to live performances and festivals.

- **Local Arts Scene**: Discover the best places to view and purchase local art.

- **Museums and Galleries**: Find out about the city's top cultural institutions.

- **Theatrical Performances**: Get information on live theater and performances.

- **Annual Events and Festivals**: Mark your calendar for Annapolis's major cultural events and festivals.

Outdoor Activities

Annapolis offers a wealth of outdoor activities, and the "Outdoor Activities" section provides information on how to enjoy them to the fullest.

- **Sailing and Boating**: Get tips on sailing, boating, and enjoying the Chesapeake Bay.

- **Parks and Nature Trails**: Find the best parks and trails for hiking, biking, and picnicking.

- **Water Sports**: Learn where to go for kayaking, paddleboarding, and other water sports.

- **Golf Courses**: Discover the best places to play a round of golf.

- **Walking Tours**: Take a guided or self-guided walking tour of the city.

Food and Drink

The "Food and Drink" section is a culinary guide to Annapolis, featuring the city's best restaurants, cafes, breweries, and more.

- **Top Restaurants**: Explore the top dining spots for various cuisines.

- **Local Cuisine**: Try Annapolis's signature dishes and local specialties.

- **Craft Breweries**: Sample local craft beers and visit popular breweries.

- **Wineries and Distilleries**: Discover local wineries and distilleries for tours and tastings.

- **Best Coffee Shops**: Find the best places for a great cup of coffee.

Shopping in Annapolis

Whether you're looking for unique souvenirs or high-end fashion, the "Shopping in Annapolis" section has you covered.

- **Historic Downtown Shops**: Shop in the historic district for unique finds.

- **Artisanal Markets**: Visit local markets for handmade goods and crafts.

- **Souvenir Shops**: Find the perfect mementos of your trip.

- **Malls and Boutiques**: Discover larger shopping centers and boutique stores.

Family-Friendly Activities

Traveling with kids? The "Family-Friendly Activities" section offers suggestions for attractions and activities that are fun for all ages.

- **Kid-Friendly Attractions**: Explore attractions that are perfect for children.

- **Educational Tours**: Find tours that combine fun and learning.

- **Family-Oriented Events**: Attend events that cater to families.

- **Parks and Playgrounds**: Locate the best parks and playgrounds for kids.

Day Trips and Excursions

Expand your adventure beyond Annapolis with the "Day Trips and Excursions" section. Discover nearby destinations worth visiting.

- **Chesapeake Bay**: Explore the natural beauty and recreational opportunities of the Chesapeake Bay.

- **St. Michaels**: Visit the charming town of St. Michaels for a day.

- **Baltimore**: Take a short trip to the bustling city of Baltimore.

- **Washington, D.C.**: Spend a day exploring the nation's capital.

- **Other Nearby Destinations**: Discover other nearby attractions and towns.

Practical Information

The "Practical Information" section provides essential tips and advice to ensure a smooth and enjoyable trip.

- **Weather and Climate**: Understand what to expect weather-wise.

- **Safety Tips**: Stay safe with these practical safety tips.

- **Health and Medical Services**: Know where to find medical help if needed.

- **Local Customs and Etiquette**: Respect local customs and etiquette.

- **Emergency Contacts**: Keep this list of important emergency contacts handy.

Resources

For additional information, the "Resources" section offers useful websites, apps, recommended reading, and local contacts to enhance your visit.

- **Useful Websites and Apps**: Find online resources and apps to help plan your trip.

- **Recommended Reading**: Dive deeper into Annapolis's history and culture with these recommended books.

- **Local Contacts**: Get in touch with local tourism offices and other helpful contacts.

Planning Your Trip

Best Time to Visit

Annapolis is a city that offers something special in every season, but the best time to visit largely depends on what you want to experience.

Spring (March to May)

Spring is a beautiful time to visit Annapolis. The city's gardens and parks are in full bloom, and the weather is mild, with temperatures ranging from the mid-50s to the low 70s (Fahrenheit). This is an ideal time for outdoor activities such as walking tours, sailing, and exploring historic sites. Spring also sees several local festivals, including the annual Annapolis Spring Sailboat Show.

Summer (June to August)

Summer is peak tourist season in Annapolis, and for good reason. The weather is warm, with temperatures often reaching the mid-80s. This is the perfect time for boating, swimming, and enjoying waterfront dining. However, it can get crowded, and accommodation prices are at their highest. The Annapolis Fourth of July celebration and the Maryland Renaissance Festival are key highlights of the summer season.

Fall (September to November)

Fall is another excellent time to visit. The weather is still pleasant, ranging from the mid-60s to mid-70s, and the summer crowds have thinned out. The city is particularly beautiful with the changing fall foliage. This is also the time for the Annapolis Boat

Shows, which draw boating enthusiasts from all over the world.

Winter (December to February)

Winter in Annapolis is quieter and can be quite charming. The temperatures can drop to the 30s and 40s, but the city's holiday decorations and events, such as the Annapolis Chocolate Binge Festival and the New Year's Annapolis celebration, add a festive atmosphere. This is also the best time to find deals on accommodations.

Getting There

Annapolis is conveniently located near major cities and transport hubs, making it accessible by various means of transportation.

By Air

The closest major airport to Annapolis is Baltimore/Washington International Thurgood Marshall Airport (BWI), which is about 25 miles away. From BWI, you can rent a car, take a shuttle, or use ride-sharing services to reach Annapolis. Alternatively, Washington Dulles International Airport (IAD) and Ronald Reagan Washington National Airport (DCA) are about 60 miles away, offering additional flight options.

By Car

Annapolis is easily accessible by car. It is located about 30 miles from Baltimore and 32 miles from Washington, D.C. Major highways such as US Route 50/301 connect Annapolis with these cities. If you're driving from New York City, it's approximately a 3.5-hour drive via I-95.

By Train

While Annapolis doesn't have its own train station, you can take an Amtrak train to BWI Airport or New Carrollton, and then transfer to a bus or taxi to reach Annapolis. MARC trains, which run between Baltimore and Washington, D.C., also stop at New Carrollton.

By Bus

Several bus services operate routes to Annapolis from nearby cities. Greyhound and Megabus offer affordable options with stops in Annapolis. Local bus services, such as the Maryland Transit Administration (MTA), also provide routes connecting Annapolis to Baltimore and Washington, D.C.

Transportation Options

Once you're in Annapolis, there are several ways to get around the city.

By Car

Having a car can be convenient, especially if you plan to explore areas outside downtown Annapolis. However, parking can be limited in the historic district. There are several parking garages and lots available, as well as street parking with metered spots.

Public Transportation

Annapolis Transit provides local bus services with routes covering key areas of the city. The buses are a reliable and affordable option for getting around. Additionally, the MTA offers regional bus services connecting Annapolis to Baltimore and Washington, D.C.

Biking

Annapolis is a bike-friendly city with several bike lanes and trails. You can rent a bike from local shops and enjoy a scenic ride through the city. The Annapolis Bicycle Club offers group rides for various skill levels.

Walking

The historic downtown area is compact and pedestrian-friendly, making walking one of the best ways to explore Annapolis. Many of the city's attractions, shops, and restaurants are within walking distance of each other.

Accommodation Guide

Annapolis offers a wide range of accommodations to suit different preferences and budgets. Here's a guide to help you choose the best place to stay.

Hotels

Annapolis has numerous hotels ranging from luxury to budget options.

- **The Westin Annapolis**: Located near the city center, The Westin offers upscale accommodations with amenities such as a fitness center, spa, and on-site dining.

- **Annapolis Waterfront Hotel**: For those wanting to stay close to the water, this hotel offers stunning views of the harbor and is within walking distance of many attractions.

- **Historic Inns of Annapolis**: These three historic inns – the Governor Calvert House, the Maryland Inn, and the Robert Johnson House

– offer charming accommodations in the heart of downtown.

- **Hampton Inn & Suites Annapolis**: A more budget-friendly option that provides comfortable accommodations and complimentary breakfast.

Bed and Breakfasts

Staying at a bed and breakfast offers a more personalized and unique experience.

- **Gibson's Lodgings**: Located near the US Naval Academy, this B&B offers comfortable rooms and a charming courtyard.

- **Scotlaur Inn Bed & Breakfast**: Situated above a popular local diner, this B&B provides a cozy and homey atmosphere.

- **Flag House Inn**: This historic inn offers elegant rooms and a convenient location near downtown attractions.

Vacation Rentals

For those seeking more space or a home-like environment, vacation rentals are a great option.

- **Airbnb**: Annapolis has a variety of Airbnb options, from apartments in the city center to waterfront homes.

- **VRBO**: Similar to Airbnb, VRBO offers a range of rental properties to suit different needs and preferences.

- **Local Agencies**: There are also local property management companies that specialize in vacation rentals in the Annapolis area.

Budgeting Your Trip

Budgeting your trip to Annapolis will depend on your travel style and preferences. Here are some tips to help you manage your expenses.

Accommodation

- **Luxury**: Expect to pay upwards of $300 per night for high-end hotels and historic inns.

- **Mid-Range**: Mid-range hotels and B&Bs typically cost between $150 to $300 per night.

- **Budget**: Budget accommodations, including motels and budget hotels, can be found for under $150 per night.

Food and Drink

- **Dining Out**: Annapolis has a diverse culinary scene. Fine dining restaurants can cost $50 or more per person, while mid-range options may cost around $20 to $40 per person. Budget-friendly eateries, including diners and fast-food options, can cost under $20 per person.

- **Local Specialties**: Don't miss trying local seafood, especially the Maryland blue crabs. Many waterfront restaurants offer seafood dishes at various price points.

Activities

- **Attractions**: Many of Annapolis's historic sites and museums charge admission fees. Expect to pay around $10 to $20 per person for entry.

- **Tours**: Guided tours, such as sailing trips or walking tours, can range from $20 to $50 per person.

- **Free Activities**: There are plenty of free things to do in Annapolis, such as exploring the historic downtown, visiting parks, and enjoying the waterfront.

Transportation

- **Public Transit**: Local bus fares are generally low, making public transportation an affordable option.

- **Car Rental**: If you plan to rent a car, budget for rental fees, gas, and parking costs.

- **Biking and Walking**: Both are cost-effective ways to get around, especially in the downtown area.

So, planning ahead and considering these factors, you can enjoy a wonderful trip to Annapolis that fits your budget and interests. Whether you're looking for luxury or traveling on a budget, Annapolis has something to offer every traveler.

Historical Overview

Early History

Annapolis, the capital of Maryland, boasts a rich history that dates back to the early 17th century. Originally inhabited by the Algonquin-speaking Native American tribes, the area was known for its fertile land and abundant waterways. The first European settlers arrived in the mid-1600s. In 1649, a group of Puritan exiles from Virginia, led by William Stone, established a settlement known as "Providence" on the north shore of the Severn River.

The settlement was initially focused on agriculture, with tobacco quickly becoming the primary cash crop. The area's growth was slow but steady, and by 1694, the settlement, then known as Anne Arundel Town, was renamed Annapolis in honor of Princess Anne, the future Queen of England. In 1695, Annapolis was officially designated as the capital of Maryland, replacing St. Mary's City. This marked the beginning of Annapolis's transformation into a significant political and cultural hub.

Colonial Annapolis

During the colonial period, Annapolis flourished as a center of politics, commerce, and education. The city's strategic location on the Chesapeake Bay made it a crucial port for trade. By the early 18th century, Annapolis had developed into a thriving town with a bustling harbor, elegant homes, and a vibrant social scene.

One of the most significant developments in colonial Annapolis was the establishment of the Maryland State House in 1772. This historic building remains the oldest state capitol in continuous legislative use and is renowned for its beautiful architecture and historical significance. The State House played a pivotal role in the American Revolution, serving as the temporary

U.S. Capitol from 1783 to 1784, where the Treaty of Paris was ratified, officially ending the Revolutionary War.

Annapolis was also home to many prominent figures of the American Revolution, including Samuel Chase, William Paca, Thomas Stone, and Charles Carroll of Carrollton, all of whom were signers of the Declaration of Independence. Their contributions to the cause of independence were instrumental in shaping the nation's future.

The social and cultural life of colonial Annapolis was vibrant. The city was known for its grand balls, horse races, and theatrical performances. The Annapolis Subscription Assembly, established in 1744, was one of the earliest organizations dedicated to social and cultural activities in the colonies. Education was also highly valued, with the founding of King William's School in 1696, which later became part of St. John's College, one of the oldest institutions of higher learning in the United States.

Annapolis in the 19th and 20th Centuries

The 19th century brought significant changes to Annapolis. The War of 1812 had a considerable impact on the city, with British forces blockading the Chesapeake Bay and threatening coastal settlements. Despite these challenges, Annapolis continued to grow and develop.

In 1845, the establishment of the United States Naval Academy marked a new era for the city. The Academy was founded to address the need for a permanent institution to train naval officers, and it quickly became a prestigious institution. The presence of the Naval Academy brought increased federal investment and a steady influx of students and visitors, contributing to the city's economic and social vitality.

The Civil War era was a tumultuous time for Annapolis. Maryland, a border state, was divided in its loyalties, and Annapolis saw both Union and Confederate sympathizers. The city was occupied by Union forces, and the Naval Academy was temporarily relocated to Newport, Rhode Island. Annapolis served as a crucial location for Union troop movements and as a hospital site for wounded soldiers.

The post-Civil War period saw Annapolis evolve into a more modern city. The introduction of railroads and improved transportation infrastructure facilitated commerce and connectivity. By the late 19th and early 20th centuries, Annapolis had become a popular destination for tourists, drawn by its historical sites, waterfront, and charming atmosphere.

The 20th century brought further modernization and growth. The Naval Academy continued to expand, and Annapolis became known as the

"Sailing Capital of the United States," attracting sailing enthusiasts from around the world. The city's historic preservation efforts gained momentum in the mid-20th century, leading to the restoration and preservation of many of its colonial-era buildings and landmarks.

Modern-Day Annapolis

Today, Annapolis is a vibrant city that honors its rich history while embracing modernity. The historic district of Annapolis is a testament to the city's colonial past, with its well-preserved 18th-century buildings and cobblestone streets. Walking through downtown Annapolis, visitors can explore a myriad of historic sites, including the Maryland State House, the William Paca House and Garden, and the Banneker-Douglass Museum, which highlights African American history in Maryland.

The United States Naval Academy remains a central part of the city's identity. Visitors can tour the Academy's beautiful campus, visit the Naval Academy Museum, and attend events such as the annual Commissioning Week, which culminates in the graduation and commissioning of new naval officers.

Annapolis's maritime heritage is celebrated through various events and activities. The Annapolis Boat Shows, held annually in the spring and fall, are among the largest and most prestigious in the world, attracting boating enthusiasts and industry professionals. The city's waterfront offers numerous opportunities for sailing, kayaking, and enjoying the scenic views of the Chesapeake Bay.

Culturally, Annapolis is a thriving community with a robust arts scene. The city hosts numerous festivals, art exhibits, and theatrical performances throughout the year. The Maryland Hall for the Creative Arts is a focal point for the local arts community, offering classes, performances, and exhibitions.

Annapolis is also known for its culinary scene, which features a diverse array of restaurants and eateries. Seafood is a highlight, with Maryland blue crabs, oysters, and rockfish being local favorites. The city's restaurants range from upscale dining establishments to casual waterfront crab shacks.

In recent years, Annapolis has embraced sustainability and environmental conservation. Efforts to protect the Chesapeake Bay and promote green initiatives are a significant part of the community's ethos. The city's commitment to preserving its natural beauty and historic charm ensures that Annapolis remains a cherished destination for future generations.

Annapolis's history is a rich tapestry of early settlement, colonial prosperity, revolutionary fervor, and modern growth. The city's ability to honor its past while evolving with the times makes it a unique and fascinating place to visit. Whether you're exploring historic landmarks, enjoying the waterfront, or immersing yourself in the local culture, Annapolis offers a timeless experience that resonates with visitors from all walks of life.

Top Attractions

Annapolis is a city brimming with history, culture, and scenic beauty. Here are some of the top attractions that should be on every visitor's list.

United States Naval Academy

The United States Naval Academy (USNA), founded in 1845, is a premier institution for educating and commissioning officers into the U.S. Navy and Marine Corps. Situated on the banks of the Severn River, the Academy's picturesque campus, known as "The Yard," is open to the public and offers a wealth of historical and educational experiences.

Key Highlights:

- **Bancroft Hall**: This is the largest single dormitory in the world, housing all midshipmen. Visitors can see the Rotunda, adorned with murals and the iconic Memorial Hall, which honors alumni who died in service.

- **Naval Academy Chapel**: This beautiful domed chapel is a prominent feature of the Academy. Beneath the chapel lies the crypt of John Paul Jones, the father of the U.S. Navy.

- **Naval Academy Museum**: Located in Preble Hall, the museum showcases a vast collection of naval artifacts, including ship models, uniforms, and historical documents.

- **Visitor Center**: Begin your visit here to watch a short film about the Academy and join a guided walking tour led by knowledgeable guides, often retired naval officers.

The Academy is not just a school; it's a living museum that offers a unique glimpse into naval history and the rigorous life of midshipmen.

Maryland State House

The Maryland State House is the oldest state capitol in continuous legislative use and a must-see for history enthusiasts. Completed in 1779, it served as the temporary U.S. Capitol from 1783 to 1784 and was the site of several pivotal moments in American history.

Key Highlights:

- **Historical Significance**: The State House was where the Treaty of Paris was ratified, ending the Revolutionary War. It was also where George Washington resigned his commission as commander-in-chief of the Continental Army.

- **Architecture**: The building's distinctive wooden dome, constructed without nails, is an architectural marvel. Inside, visitors can admire the elegant rotunda and chambers.

- **Exhibits**: Various exhibits detail Maryland's legislative history and its role in the founding of the United States. The Old Senate Chamber, restored to its 1783 appearance, is particularly noteworthy.

The Maryland State House offers a rich educational experience, blending history, politics, and architecture in a single visit.

Historic Downtown Annapolis

Historic Downtown Annapolis is a charming area filled with colonial architecture, cobblestone streets, and vibrant shops and restaurants. This area reflects the city's rich past and lively present.

Key Highlights:

- **Main Street**: Lined with boutique shops, galleries, and eateries, Main Street is the perfect place to stroll, shop, and dine.

- **Ego Alley**: This narrow waterway is a popular spot to watch boats dock and depart. The waterfront area is also home to several seafood restaurants offering delicious local cuisine.

- **Market House**: A historic market building offering a variety of local foods, from fresh seafood to baked goods.

- **Tours**: Consider joining a walking tour to learn more about the history and architecture of the area. Ghost tours, which delve into the haunted history of Annapolis, are also popular.

Exploring Historic Downtown Annapolis allows visitors to immerse themselves in the city's colonial charm while enjoying modern amenities.

William Paca House and Garden

The William Paca House and Garden is a beautifully restored 18th-century Georgian mansion once home to William Paca, a signer of the Declaration of Independence. This National Historic Landmark offers a glimpse into colonial life and the elegance of the period.

Key Highlights:

- **The House**: The mansion has been meticulously restored to its original grandeur. Guided tours take visitors through the richly furnished rooms, offering insights into the life of William Paca and the history of the era.

- **The Gardens**: The two-acre garden is a highlight, featuring formal terraces, a fish-shaped pond, and a charming summer house. The garden has been restored to its 18th-century layout and is a beautiful spot to relax and enjoy the landscape.

- **Events**: The house and garden host various events throughout the year, including historical reenactments, garden parties, and educational programs.

The William Paca House and Garden is a testament to Annapolis's colonial heritage, offering a serene and educational experience.

Banneker-Douglass Museum

The Banneker-Douglass Museum is Maryland's official museum of African American heritage. Named after Benjamin Banneker and Frederick Douglass, the museum highlights the contributions and achievements of African Americans in Maryland and beyond.

Key Highlights:

- **Exhibits**: The museum features permanent and rotating exhibits that cover a wide range of topics, from slavery and civil rights to contemporary African American culture.

- **The Building**: The museum is housed in the historic Mount Moriah African Methodist Episcopal Church, adding to its cultural and historical significance.

- **Programs and Events**: The museum hosts lectures, workshops, and community events aimed at educating the public and celebrating African American history and culture.

The Banneker-Douglass Museum offers a profound and engaging exploration of African American history, making it an essential visit for understanding the broader historical context of Maryland and the United States.

Annapolis Maritime Museum

The Annapolis Maritime Museum is dedicated to preserving and celebrating the maritime heritage of Annapolis and the Chesapeake Bay. Located in a historic waterman's building, the museum offers interactive exhibits and educational programs that highlight the region's maritime culture.

Key Highlights:

- **Exhibits**: The museum's exhibits cover various aspects of maritime history, including the ecology of the Chesapeake Bay, the history of oyster harvesting, and the life of watermen. Interactive displays and artifacts make the exhibits engaging for all ages.

- **The Thomas Point Shoal Lighthouse**: The museum offers tours to this iconic Chesapeake Bay lighthouse, the last remaining screw-pile lighthouse in its original location.

- **Educational Programs**: The museum runs a variety of educational programs for children and adults, including environmental education, sailing programs, and heritage tours.

- **Waterfront Views:** The museum's waterfront location offers stunning views of the Bay and is a great spot for a leisurely visit.

The Annapolis Maritime Museum provides an in-depth look at the city's connection to the Chesapeake Bay, offering both historical insights and contemporary environmental education.

Summary

Annapolis's top attractions offer a rich tapestry of experiences that cater to history enthusiasts, culture lovers, and those looking to enjoy the scenic beauty of the Chesapeake Bay. From the storied halls of the United States Naval Academy and the Maryland State House to the charming streets of Historic Downtown Annapolis and the serene gardens of the William Paca House, there is something for everyone. The Banneker-Douglass Museum provides crucial insights into African American heritage, while the Annapolis Maritime Museum celebrates the city's enduring maritime culture. Each of these attractions contributes to the unique charm and historical depth of Annapolis, making it a destination well worth exploring.

William Paca House and Garden.

Cultural Experiences

Annapolis is a city steeped in history and brimming with cultural vitality. Its local arts scene, diverse museums and galleries, theatrical performances, and annual events and festivals make it a vibrant destination for both residents and visitors. Here's an in-depth look at the cultural experiences you can enjoy in Annapolis.

Local Arts Scene

The local arts scene in Annapolis is thriving, offering a rich tapestry of visual arts, music, and performing arts that reflect the city's creative spirit.

Visual Arts

Annapolis is home to numerous galleries and art studios that showcase the works of local and regional artists. The Annapolis Arts District, located in the heart of the city, is a hub for

53 | ANNAPOLIS TRAVEL GUIDE

creativity and innovation. Here, you can find a variety of art forms, including painting, sculpture, photography, and mixed media.

- **Maryland Federation of Art (MFA) Circle Gallery**: The MFA Circle Gallery hosts rotating exhibitions featuring contemporary works by artists from Maryland and beyond. The gallery's juried exhibitions attract a wide range of high-quality submissions, providing a diverse and dynamic viewing experience.

- **ArtFarm Studios**: ArtFarm Studios offers a unique blend of gallery space and creative workshops. It's a great place to view and purchase art, as well as participate in classes ranging from drawing and painting to digital arts and crafts.

- **McBride Gallery**: This gallery represents over 70 artists and showcases a wide variety of fine art, including oils, watercolors, pastels, and sculpture. The gallery hosts several themed exhibitions throughout the year, highlighting different aspects of the artistic world.

Music and Performing Arts

Music is an integral part of the Annapolis cultural scene. The city hosts numerous live music venues, ranging from intimate coffee shops to larger concert halls.

- **Rams Head On Stage**: Known for its cozy atmosphere and exceptional acoustics, Rams Head On Stage is one of the top live music venues in the region. It hosts an eclectic mix of artists, from local musicians to nationally recognized performers, covering genres like rock, jazz, folk, and blues.

- **Maryland Hall for the Creative Arts**: This multi-disciplinary arts center offers performances, exhibitions, and classes in a variety of artistic disciplines. Maryland Hall hosts concerts, dance performances, and theatrical productions, making it a cornerstone of Annapolis's cultural life.

Museums and Galleries

Annapolis boasts a variety of museums and galleries that provide insights into the city's rich history and cultural heritage. Each museum offers unique exhibits that cater to different interests.

Historic and Cultural Museums

- **Historic Annapolis Museum**: Located in the heart of the historic district, this museum offers exhibits that chronicle the city's history from its colonial origins to the present day. Interactive displays and artifacts provide an engaging educational experience for visitors of all ages.

- **Banneker-Douglass Museum**: As Maryland's official museum of African American heritage, the Banneker-Douglass Museum highlights the contributions of African

Americans to the state's history. The museum features permanent and rotating exhibits, educational programs, and special events.

- **Chase-Lloyd House**: This Georgian-style mansion, built in the 18th century, offers guided tours that delve into the life of Samuel Chase, a signer of the Declaration of Independence. The house is beautifully preserved, with period furnishings and artifacts.

Art Galleries

- **MFA Circle Gallery**: Beyond its regular exhibitions, the MFA Circle Gallery also offers art classes and workshops, making it a vibrant community space for both viewing and creating art.

- **49 West Coffeehouse, Winebar & Gallery**: This unique venue combines a coffeehouse, wine bar, and art gallery. It regularly hosts art exhibitions, live music performances, and poetry readings, creating a dynamic cultural atmosphere.

Theatrical Performances

The theatrical scene in Annapolis is diverse and vibrant, with performances ranging from classic plays to contemporary productions.

Local Theatres

- **Colonial Players of Annapolis**: This community theater group has been producing high-quality performances since 1949. The Colonial Players offer a diverse season of plays and musicals, with productions staged in their intimate theater in downtown Annapolis. Their repertoire includes everything from modern dramas to classic comedies.

- **Compass Rose Theater**: Known for its professional-quality productions, Compass Rose Theater stages a mix of classic and contemporary plays and musicals. The theater also offers educational programs, including acting classes and summer camps for children and teens.

- **Annapolis Summer Garden Theatre**: This open-air theater presents musicals in a picturesque setting near the City Dock. The summer season typically features popular musicals, providing an enjoyable experience for theater-goers of all ages.

Performance Venues

- **Maryland Hall for the Creative Arts**: In addition to concerts, Maryland Hall hosts theatrical performances, including plays, dance productions, and operas. The venue's diverse programming ensures there's something for everyone to enjoy.

- **Rams Head On Stage**: While primarily a music venue, Rams Head On Stage occasionally hosts comedic performances, making it a versatile space for various forms of live entertainment.

Annual Events and Festivals

Annapolis hosts a plethora of annual events and festivals that celebrate the city's heritage, culture, and community spirit. These events draw visitors from near and far and provide memorable experiences.

Maritime Festivals

- **Annapolis Boat Shows**: These world-renowned boat shows, held in the spring and fall, are major events in the maritime community. The United States Powerboat Show and the United States Sailboat Show attract boating enthusiasts from around the globe. Attendees can explore a vast array of boats, marine equipment, and accessories, and enjoy seminars and demonstrations.

- **Maryland Seafood Festival**: Held annually at Sandy Point State Park, this festival celebrates the Chesapeake Bay's rich seafood heritage. Visitors can enjoy delicious seafood dishes, cooking demonstrations, live music, and family-friendly activities.

Cultural and Music Festivals

- **Annapolis Arts Week**: This week-long celebration of the arts features gallery exhibitions, live performances, workshops, and art markets. Annapolis Arts Week highlights the city's vibrant arts community and provides opportunities for visitors to engage with local artists.

- **First Sunday Arts Festival**: Held on the first Sunday of each month from May through November, this festival transforms West Street into an open-air arts market. Local artists and craftspeople display and sell their creations, and the event also features live music, street performances, and food vendors.

- **Annapolis Film Festival**: This annual event showcases independent films from around the world. The festival includes screenings, panel discussions, and workshops, providing a platform for filmmakers and a rich experience for cinema enthusiasts.

Historical Celebrations

- **Maryland Day**: Celebrated in March, Maryland Day commemorates the founding of the Maryland colony. Annapolis hosts a variety of events, including historical reenactments, tours, and educational programs.

- **Annapolis Independence Day Celebration**: The city's Fourth of July celebration includes a patriotic parade, live music, and a spectacular fireworks display over the harbor.

Annapolis's cultural scene is a vibrant tapestry that reflects the city's rich history and dynamic present. Whether you're exploring local art galleries, enjoying a theatrical performance, or participating in one of the city's many festivals, Annapolis offers a wealth of cultural experiences. From the artistic treasures of the Annapolis Arts District to the historic charm of its museums and theaters, there is something to captivate and inspire every visitor. Embrace the cultural richness of Annapolis and discover why it remains a beloved destination for those seeking a deep connection to history, art, and community.

Outdoor Activities

Annapolis, known as the "Sailing Capital of the United States," offers a myriad of outdoor activities that cater to all interests. From sailing and boating to exploring parks, nature trails, and golf courses, Annapolis provides plenty of opportunities to enjoy the great outdoors. Here's a detailed guide to the best outdoor activities in Annapolis.

Sailing and Boating

Given its prime location on the Chesapeake Bay, sailing and boating are integral parts of the Annapolis experience. Whether you're an experienced sailor or a novice, there are plenty of ways to get out on the water.

Sailing

- **Annapolis Sailing School**: Established in 1959, this school is one of the oldest and most respected sailing schools in the country. It offers courses for all skill levels, from beginner to advanced. Classes cover essential sailing techniques, navigation, and safety.

- **Schooner Woodwind**: Experience sailing on the Chesapeake Bay aboard this beautiful 74-foot schooner. The Schooner Woodwind offers two-hour public cruises, where you can participate in raising the sails or just relax and enjoy the view. Private charters are also available for a more personalized experience.

- **Sailboat Rentals**: If you prefer to sail on your own, several companies in Annapolis offer sailboat rentals. Annapolis Bay Charters and Annapolis Boat Rentals provide a range of boats for daily or hourly rental.

Boating

- **Powerboat Rentals**: For those who prefer powerboating, there are numerous rental options available. South River Boat Rentals and Chesapeake Bay Sport Fishing offer a variety of powerboats for rent, allowing you to explore the bay at your own pace.

- **Kayaking and Paddleboarding**: Annapolis is an excellent location for kayaking and paddleboarding. Chesapeake Light Craft and Capital SUP offer rentals and guided tours, providing a unique perspective of the city from the water.

- **Annapolis Harbor**: The bustling Annapolis Harbor is a great place to watch boats come and go. Ego Alley, a narrow waterway in the harbor, is a popular spot where boaters show off their vessels. Docking at Ego Alley is an event in itself, attracting both boaters and spectators.

Parks and Nature Trails

Annapolis is home to several parks and nature trails that offer beautiful landscapes and a variety of outdoor activities.

Quiet Waters Park

Located on the South River, Quiet Waters Park is a 340-acre oasis that offers a range of activities:

- **Trails**: The park features over six miles of paved trails for walking, jogging, and biking. The trails meander through forests and open meadows, providing scenic views of the river.

- **Dog Park**: Quiet Waters has two dog parks where dogs can run off-leash. There's also a dog beach where pets can swim in the river.

- **Art Galleries**: The park is home to two art galleries that showcase local artists. The galleries host rotating exhibitions, providing a cultural element to your outdoor experience.

- **Picnicking and Playgrounds**: There are several picnic areas with tables and grills, as well as playgrounds for children.

Sandy Point State Park

Situated on the Chesapeake Bay, Sandy Point State Park is a popular destination for swimming, fishing, and picnicking:

- **Beaches**: The park has a large sandy beach with designated swimming areas. Lifeguards are on duty during the summer months.

- **Fishing and Crabbing**: The park's fishing pier and designated crabbing areas are great spots for catching local seafood.

- **Trails**: Sandy Point offers several trails, including a scenic route that provides views of the Bay Bridge.

- **Boat Rentals**: Kayaks, paddleboards, and other small boats are available for rent, allowing you to explore the bay waters.

Greenbury Point Nature Center

Greenbury Point is a nature lover's paradise, offering a mix of forest, wetlands, and open fields:

- **Trails**: The center has several trails that are perfect for hiking and birdwatching. The Tower Trail offers stunning views of the Severn River and the Chesapeake Bay.

- **Wildlife Viewing**: The diverse habitats support a variety of wildlife, including deer, foxes, and numerous bird species.

Water Sports

Annapolis's location on the Chesapeake Bay makes it an ideal spot for a variety of water sports.

Kayaking and Paddleboarding

- **Capital SUP**: Located on Spa Creek, Capital SUP offers kayak and paddleboard rentals, lessons, and guided tours. Their eco-tours provide a unique way to explore the local waterways and learn about the area's ecology.

- **Kayak Annapolis**: This company offers guided kayak tours of Annapolis, including sunset and moonlight paddles. Tours are suitable for all skill levels and provide a unique perspective of the city's historic waterfront.

Jet Skiing and Parasailing

- **Annapolis Watersports**: For those seeking a thrill, Annapolis Watersports offers jet ski rentals and parasailing adventures. Experience the exhilaration of speeding across the bay or soaring high above it for a bird's-eye view of the city.

- **Chesapeake Beach Resort & Spa**: Located a short drive from Annapolis, this resort offers jet ski rentals and parasailing trips, making it a great day trip option.

Golf Courses

Golf enthusiasts will find several top-notch courses in and around Annapolis.

The Golf Club at South River

- **Course**: This private club features an 18-hole championship course designed by renowned architect Brian Ault. The course is known for its challenging layout and scenic views.

- **Amenities**: The club offers a full range of amenities, including a driving range, practice greens, and a clubhouse with dining facilities.

Annapolis Golf Club

- **Course**: Annapolis Golf Club is a public 18-hole course that offers a relaxed and friendly atmosphere. The course is relatively short, making it a good choice for beginners and those looking for a casual round.

- **Facilities**: The club has a pro shop and snack bar, and offers golf lessons for all skill levels.

Eisenhower Golf Course

- **Course**: Named after President Dwight D. Eisenhower, this public course offers a challenging 18-hole layout that winds through wooded terrain. The course has been recently renovated, with new bunkers, greens, and fairways.

- **Facilities**: The course features a driving range, practice green, and a clubhouse with a restaurant and bar.

Walking Tours

Exploring Annapolis on foot is a fantastic way to experience the city's rich history and charming streets. There are several guided walking tours available that cater to different interests.

Historic Walking Tours

- **Historic Annapolis Foundation**: This organization offers guided tours of the historic district, including visits to landmarks such as the Maryland State House, St. Anne's Church, and the William Paca House. Knowledgeable guides provide insights into the city's colonial past and significant historical events.

- **Watermark Tours**: Watermark offers a variety of walking tours, including the popular "Four Centuries Walking Tour," which covers the city's history from its founding to the present day. They also offer themed tours, such as the "Haunted Harbor Ghost Walk."

Specialty Tours

- **African American Heritage Tour**: This tour, offered by the Banneker-Douglass Museum, explores the history and contributions of African Americans in Annapolis. The tour includes visits to important sites and landmarks, such as the Thurgood Marshall Memorial and the Kunta Kinte-Alex Haley Memorial.

- **Culinary Tours**: Annapolis Food Tours offers walking tours that combine history with culinary delights. Participants can sample local cuisine at various restaurants and learn about the city's food culture.

Self-Guided Tours

For those who prefer to explore at their own pace, self-guided walking tour maps are available from the Annapolis Visitor Center. These maps highlight key attractions and provide historical context, allowing visitors to create their own personalized tour.

Annapolis's outdoor activities offer something for everyone, whether you're a water sports enthusiast, a nature lover, a golf aficionado, or a history buff. From the thrill of sailing on the Chesapeake Bay to the tranquility of walking through historic parks and trails, Annapolis provides countless opportunities to enjoy the great outdoors. Embrace the natural beauty and rich history of Annapolis through these engaging and diverse outdoor experiences.

Food and Drink

Annapolis offers a culinary landscape as diverse and rich as its history. Whether you're craving fine dining, local specialties, craft brews, or a perfect cup of coffee, Annapolis has something to satisfy every palate. Here's a detailed guide to the food and drink scene in this vibrant city.

Top Restaurants

Annapolis boasts a wide array of restaurants, ranging from upscale dining to casual eateries. Here are some top recommendations:

Fine Dining

- **Reynolds Tavern**: Housed in a historic 18th-century building, Reynolds Tavern offers a refined dining experience. The menu features American and European-inspired dishes with a modern twist. Afternoon tea is a highlight, served in the elegant tea room or garden.

- **Carrol's Creek Café**: Located on the waterfront, Carrol's Creek Café offers stunning views of the harbor along with its upscale menu. Specializing in seafood, the restaurant is known for its crab cakes, fresh oysters, and creative entrees.

- **Lewnes' Steakhouse**: A family-owned establishment, Lewnes' Steakhouse is a classic choice for steak lovers. Known for its prime cuts of beef and extensive wine list, it offers a traditional steakhouse atmosphere with top-notch service.

Casual Dining

- **Boatyard Bar & Grill**: A local favorite, Boatyard Bar & Grill is the place to go for casual dining and great seafood. The crab cakes, fish tacos, and steamed shrimp are must-tries. The laid-back atmosphere and nautical décor add to the charm.

- **Miss Shirley's Café**: Famous for its breakfast and brunch, Miss Shirley's Café offers a menu filled with Southern-inspired comfort food. The crab hash and chicken and waffles are particularly popular, and the café's welcoming vibe makes it a great spot for families.

- **Federal House Bar & Grille**: Located in a historic building, Federal House Bar & Grille serves classic American fare with a focus on local ingredients. Their extensive menu includes everything from burgers to seafood, and the outdoor patio is perfect for people-watching.

Local Cuisine

Annapolis's local cuisine is deeply rooted in its maritime heritage, with seafood being a standout feature. Here are some local specialties you should not miss:

Maryland Blue Crabs

- **Steamed Crabs**: A visit to Annapolis wouldn't be complete without experiencing a crab feast. Many local seafood shacks and restaurants offer steamed blue crabs, seasoned with Old Bay and served with melted butter.

- **Crab Cakes**: Annapolis is renowned for its crab cakes, often made with lump crabmeat and minimal filler to let the sweet, delicate flavor of the crab shine. Many restaurants, like **Carrol's**

Creek Café and **Boatyard Bar & Grill**, offer their own signature versions.

Oysters

- **Raw Oysters**: The Chesapeake Bay is home to some of the best oysters in the country. Raw bars, such as **The Choptank**, serve fresh, briny oysters on the half shell, often with a variety of sauces.

- **Oyster Stew**: This creamy, savory dish is a local favorite, especially during the colder months. It's typically made with fresh oysters, cream, butter, and spices.

Rockfish

- **Grilled or Blackened Rockfish**: Also known as striped bass, rockfish is another local delicacy. It's commonly grilled or blackened and served with seasonal vegetables and savory sauces. **Cantler's Riverside Inn** is a popular spot for trying this dish.

Craft Breweries

The craft beer scene in Annapolis has been growing steadily, with several breweries offering unique and flavorful brews.

- **Annapolis Brewing Company**: Located in the heart of downtown, this brewery offers a variety of craft beers, from IPAs to stouts. Their rotating taps ensure there's always something new to try. The brewery's cozy atmosphere makes it a great spot to relax and enjoy a pint.

- **Forward Brewing**: Situated in the Eastport neighborhood, Forward Brewing is known for its innovative beers and community-focused vibe. They offer a range of brews, including hoppy IPAs, crisp lagers, and rich porters. The brewery also emphasizes sustainability and local sourcing.

- **Crooked Crab Brewing Company**: Located in nearby Odenton, Crooked Crab Brewing

Company is worth the short drive from Annapolis. They offer a wide range of craft beers, including the popular High Joltage Double IPA and the delightfully tart Raspberry White.

- **Evo Public House**: While a bit farther afield in Salisbury, Evo Public House, part of Evolution Craft Brewing Company, is a favorite among craft beer enthusiasts. Their Primal Pale Ale and Lot No. 3 IPA are highly recommended.

Wineries and Distilleries

The Annapolis area is also home to several wineries and distilleries, offering a taste of local craftsmanship.

- **Great Frogs Winery**: Located just outside Annapolis, Great Frogs Winery offers a rustic, vineyard experience. Their handcrafted wines, made from locally grown grapes, include robust reds, crisp whites, and refreshing rosés. The winery offers tastings and tours, and the scenic vineyard is perfect for a relaxing afternoon.

- **Blackwater Distilling & Tavern**: This local distillery produces a range of craft spirits, including vodka, rum, and whiskey. Their flagship product, Sloop Betty Vodka, is particularly popular. The distillery offers tours and tastings, providing insight into their artisanal production process.

- **Lyon Distilling Company**: Situated in St. Michaels, a short drive from Annapolis, Lyon Distilling Company specializes in small-batch rum and whiskey. Their rum, crafted with molasses and sugar cane, is a standout, and their tasting room offers a variety of samples.

Best Coffee Shops

For coffee lovers, Annapolis has several excellent coffee shops that provide the perfect spot to relax, work, or catch up with friends.

- **Bean Rush Café**: With locations in both Annapolis and Crownsville, Bean Rush Café is a favorite among locals. They offer a wide range of coffee drinks, from expertly brewed espressos to refreshing iced coffees. Their pastries and sandwiches are also worth trying.

- **City Dock Coffee**: Situated near the waterfront, City Dock Coffee is a great place to grab a cup of joe while enjoying views of the harbor. Their extensive menu includes classic coffee drinks, as well as unique options like the Annapolis Fog (a twist on the London Fog).

- **Ceremony Coffee Roasters**: Known for their high-quality beans and meticulous brewing methods, Ceremony Coffee Roasters is a must-visit for coffee aficionados. They offer a variety of single-origin coffees and blends, as well as espresso-based drinks. The modern, airy space is perfect for enjoying your coffee.

- **Rise Up Coffee**: With a commitment to organic, fair-trade coffee, Rise Up Coffee has become a popular spot in Annapolis. Their cold brew is particularly popular, and their friendly, laid-back atmosphere makes it a great place to unwind.

- **Brown Mustache Coffee**: Located within the Old Fox Books shop, Brown Mustache Coffee offers a cozy and eclectic setting. Enjoy a book while sipping on a perfectly crafted latte or cappuccino.

Annapolis's food and drink scene is a delightful reflection of its rich heritage and vibrant community. From savoring fresh seafood at waterfront restaurants to exploring local breweries, wineries, and coffee shops, there are endless opportunities to indulge in the city's culinary offerings. Whether you're a foodie looking for the next great meal or a casual diner seeking a cozy café, Annapolis has something to satisfy every taste. Enjoy the diverse and delicious experiences that this charming city has to offer.

Shopping in Annapolis

Annapolis is a shopper's paradise, offering a delightful blend of historic charm and modern flair. From the quaint streets of Historic Downtown to the vibrant artisanal markets and contemporary malls, Annapolis provides a diverse shopping experience. Here's a detailed guide to the best shopping destinations in the city.

Historic Downtown Shops

Historic Downtown Annapolis is a treasure trove of unique boutiques, antique stores, and specialty shops. Walking through the cobblestone streets, you'll find a variety of stores offering everything from local crafts to high-end fashion.

Main Street and Maryland Avenue

- **The Annapolis Pottery**: Established in 1969, this charming shop offers a wide selection of handcrafted pottery. From functional kitchenware to decorative pieces, the Annapolis Pottery is perfect for finding a unique gift or souvenir.

- **Chesapeake Trading Company**: Located on Main Street, this store specializes in nautical-themed gifts and home decor. It's an excellent place to find items that capture the spirit of Annapolis and the Chesapeake Bay.

- **Zachary's Jewelers**: This family-owned jeweler is renowned for its exquisite selection of fine jewelry, including custom designs and exclusive collections. Whether you're looking for a special gift or a piece to commemorate your visit, Zachary's Jewelers offers timeless elegance.

- **Old Fox Books & Coffeehouse**: Combining a cozy coffee shop with a charming bookstore, Old Fox Books is a haven for book lovers. Browse through a curated selection of new and used books while enjoying a cup of locally roasted coffee.

- **Rams Head on Stage Gift Shop**: Located within the famous live music venue, this shop offers music-themed merchandise, including concert posters, apparel, and accessories. It's a great place to pick up a memento from your visit to this iconic venue.

Maryland Avenue

- **Mills Fine Wine & Spirits**: Established in 1937, this historic store offers a vast selection of fine wines, craft beers, and premium spirits. The knowledgeable staff can help you find the perfect bottle for any occasion.

- **Laura's Eyes**: This boutique specializes in designer eyewear and accessories. With a wide range of frames from top brands, Laura's Eyes offers stylish options for every taste.

- **The Annapolis Bookstore**: Nestled on Maryland Avenue, this independent bookstore features a carefully curated selection of new and used books, as well as unique literary gifts. The cozy atmosphere and friendly staff make it a must-visit for book enthusiasts.

Artisanal Markets

Annapolis's artisanal markets are a vibrant part of the city's shopping scene, offering handmade goods, fresh produce, and local specialties. These markets provide a unique opportunity to support local artisans and farmers while discovering one-of-a-kind items.

The Annapolis Market House

The historic Annapolis Market House, located near City Dock, has been a central part of the city's commercial life since the 18th century. Recently renovated, the Market House now hosts a variety of vendors offering fresh, local products.

- **Local Produce**: Fresh fruits, vegetables, and herbs from local farms.

- **Artisan Foods**: Gourmet cheeses, baked goods, and specialty foods.

- **Crafts and Gifts**: Handcrafted jewelry, pottery, and other artisanal products.

The Market House is a great place to sample local flavors and find unique gifts to take home.

Annapolis Farmers Market

Held at the Riva Road location, the Annapolis Farmers Market is a popular spot for locals and visitors alike.

- **Seasonal Produce**: Fresh, seasonal fruits and vegetables from local farms.
- **Handmade Goods**: Crafts, soaps, candles, and other handmade items.
- **Prepared Foods**: Freshly baked bread, pastries, and other prepared foods.

The market operates from early spring through late fall, providing a lively and vibrant shopping experience.

Souvenir Shops

Finding the perfect souvenir to remember your trip to Annapolis is easy with the variety of souvenir shops available. These stores offer a range of items that capture the essence of the city.

- **Annapolis Maritime Antiques**: This store specializes in authentic maritime antiques and nautical decor. Items include vintage ship wheels, lanterns, and other maritime artifacts that make for unique souvenirs.

- **Navy Gear**: Located near the United States Naval Academy, Navy Gear offers a wide selection of Navy-themed apparel, accessories, and gifts. It's an excellent place to find souvenirs that celebrate Annapolis's naval heritage.

- **A.L. Goodies General Store**: This classic general store offers a variety of Annapolis-themed gifts, including T-shirts, hats, mugs, and postcards. The nostalgic atmosphere and friendly service make it a fun place to shop.

Malls and Boutiques

For a more contemporary shopping experience, Annapolis offers several malls and boutiques that cater to a variety of tastes and budgets.

Westfield Annapolis Mall

Westfield Annapolis Mall is the largest shopping center in the area, featuring a wide range of stores, dining options, and entertainment.

- **Department Stores**: Major retailers like Nordstrom and Macy's offer a comprehensive shopping experience with a wide range of products.

- **Fashion Boutiques**: Stores like Anthropologie, J.Crew, and Lululemon provide the latest in fashion and activewear.

- **Specialty Shops**: From electronics at the Apple Store to beauty products at Sephora, the mall offers a diverse selection of specialty stores.

The mall also features a variety of dining options, from fast food to sit-down restaurants, and a movie theater for entertainment.

Annapolis Towne Centre

Annapolis Towne Centre is a modern shopping destination with a mix of retail stores, restaurants, and entertainment venues.

- **Fashion and Accessories**: Boutiques like South Moon Under and Anthropologie offer trendy clothing and accessories.

- **Home Goods**: Stores like Arhaus and Sur La Table provide stylish home furnishings and kitchenware.

- **Dining**: The Towne Centre offers a range of dining options, including upscale restaurants like Cooper's Hawk Winery & Restaurant and casual spots like P.F. Chang's.

Shopping in Annapolis offers a delightful blend of historic charm and modern convenience. From the unique boutiques and antique stores in Historic Downtown to the vibrant artisanal markets and contemporary malls, there's something for every shopper. Whether you're looking for a special souvenir, the latest fashion, or a unique piece of local art, Annapolis provides a diverse and enjoyable shopping experience. Embrace the charm and variety of Annapolis's shopping destinations and discover why this city is a favorite among visitors and locals alike.

Family-Friendly Activities

Annapolis is an excellent destination for families, offering a variety of activities that cater to all ages. From engaging kid-friendly attractions and educational tours to family-oriented events and beautiful parks and playgrounds, Annapolis provides plenty of opportunities for families to bond and create lasting memories. Here's a detailed guide to the best family-friendly activities in Annapolis.

Kid-Friendly Attractions

Annapolis boasts several attractions that are perfect for children, providing fun and educational experiences.

Annapolis Maritime Museum & Park

The Annapolis Maritime Museum & Park offers interactive exhibits and hands-on activities that educate visitors about the maritime heritage of Annapolis and the Chesapeake Bay.

- **Interactive Exhibits**: Kids can explore the Bay through interactive exhibits that teach them about the local ecosystem, oyster harvesting, and the history of maritime trade.

- **Touch Tank**: The museum's touch tank allows children to get up close with Chesapeake Bay marine life, including crabs, fish, and other sea creatures.

- **Summer Camps**: The museum offers summer camps that provide educational and fun activities focused on marine science and environmental conservation.

Pirate Adventures on the Chesapeake

Pirate Adventures on the Chesapeake offers an exciting and imaginative experience for young pirates.

- **Pirate Ship Cruises**: Kids can dress up as pirates and embark on a swashbuckling adventure aboard a pirate ship. The interactive cruise includes a treasure hunt, face painting, and water cannon battles.

- **Birthday Parties**: The pirate ship also offers birthday party packages, making it a memorable place to celebrate a special occasion.

Chesapeake Children's Museum

The Chesapeake Children's Museum provides a hands-on learning environment where kids can explore and discover.

- **Interactive Exhibits**: The museum features exhibits on topics such as wildlife, the environment, and local history. Kids can engage in activities like dressing up as firefighters, playing in the pretend grocery store, and exploring nature trails.

- **Workshops and Programs**: The museum offers various workshops and programs that focus on science, art, and nature, providing enriching experiences for children of all ages.

Educational Tours

Annapolis offers a variety of educational tours that are both informative and entertaining for families.

United States Naval Academy Tour

A tour of the United States Naval Academy is a must-do for families visiting Annapolis.

- **Guided Tours**: The guided tours provide insights into the history and traditions of the Naval Academy. Highlights include visits to the

Naval Academy Chapel, Bancroft Hall, and the John Paul Jones Crypt.

- **Visitor Center**: The Armel-Leftwich Visitor Center features exhibits on the history of the Academy, interactive displays, and a gift shop.

Historic Annapolis Walking Tour

The Historic Annapolis Walking Tour offers a fascinating journey through the city's rich history.

- **Guided Tours**: Knowledgeable guides lead visitors through the historic district, sharing stories about the city's colonial past, significant landmarks, and notable figures.

- **Family-Friendly Focus**: The tour is designed to be engaging for all ages, making history come alive for children and adults alike.

Maryland State House Tour

The Maryland State House, the oldest state capitol in continuous legislative use, offers educational tours that provide insights into Maryland's political history.

- **Guided and Self-Guided Tours**: Families can choose between guided tours led by knowledgeable docents or self-guided tours with informational brochures.

- **Historical Exhibits**: The State House features exhibits on Maryland's history, including the Revolutionary War and the Civil War, making it an educational experience for children.

Family-Oriented Events

Annapolis hosts a variety of family-oriented events throughout the year, providing fun and entertainment for all ages.

Annapolis Spring Sailboat Show

The Annapolis Spring Sailboat Show is a family-friendly event that celebrates sailing and boating.

- **Boat Tours and Demonstrations**: Families can tour a variety of sailboats and participate in sailing demonstrations.

- **Kid's Zone**: The event features a dedicated Kid's Zone with activities such as face painting, boat-building workshops, and interactive games.

First Sunday Arts Festival

Held on the first Sunday of each month from May through November, the First Sunday Arts Festival is a vibrant event that features local artists, musicians, and performers.

- **Art and Craft Vendors**: Families can browse booths selling handmade crafts, jewelry, and artwork.

- **Live Performances**: The festival includes live music and street performances that entertain visitors of all ages.

- **Food Vendors**: A variety of food vendors offer delicious treats, making it a fun outing for the whole family.

Maryland Renaissance Festival

The Maryland Renaissance Festival, held annually from late August through October, transports visitors back to the 16th century with its medieval-themed entertainment.

- **Costumed Performers**: The festival features costumed performers, including knights, jesters, and musicians, who bring the Renaissance period to life.

- **Family Activities**: Kids can enjoy activities such as pony rides, archery, and crafts. The festival also includes stage shows, jousting tournaments, and delicious food.

Parks and Playgrounds

Annapolis is home to numerous parks and playgrounds that offer outdoor recreation and fun for families.

Quiet Waters Park

Quiet Waters Park is a 340-acre park that offers a variety of recreational activities.

- **Playgrounds**: The park features multiple playgrounds with equipment for children of all ages.

- **Trails**: Families can enjoy walking, biking, or jogging on the park's paved trails, which wind through scenic wooded areas and open meadows.

- **Picnic Areas**: There are several picnic areas with tables and grills, making it a great spot for a family picnic.

- **Dog Park**: The park includes a dog park where families can bring their furry friends for some off-leash fun.

Truxtun Park

Truxtun Park is a popular destination for outdoor activities and sports.

- **Playgrounds**: The park has playgrounds with swings, slides, and climbing structures that are perfect for children.

- **Sports Facilities**: Truxtun Park features tennis courts, baseball fields, and a skate park, providing a variety of recreational options for families.

- **Swimming Pool**: During the summer months, the park's swimming pool is a great place for families to cool off and have fun.

Jonas Green Park

Located along the Severn River, Jonas Green Park offers beautiful views and outdoor activities.

- **Fishing Pier**: The park's fishing pier is a popular spot for families to fish and enjoy the water.

- **Trails**: The park has walking and biking trails that provide scenic views of the river and surrounding nature.

- **Picnic Areas**: There are picnic areas with tables and grills, making it a lovely spot for a family outing.

Annapolis offers a wealth of family-friendly activities that cater to children and adults alike. From engaging kid-friendly attractions and educational tours to fun-filled family events and beautiful parks and playgrounds, Annapolis provides endless opportunities for families to explore, learn, and have fun together.

Day Trips and Excursions

Annapolis is perfectly situated for exploring the surrounding region, offering a variety of exciting day trip options. Whether you're interested in nature, history, or urban adventures, there's something for everyone within a short drive. Here's a detailed guide to the best day trips and excursions from Annapolis.

Chesapeake Bay

The Chesapeake Bay is the largest estuary in the United States and offers numerous opportunities for outdoor recreation and exploration.

Activities

- **Boating and Sailing**: The Chesapeake Bay is a boater's paradise. Consider renting a sailboat or powerboat to explore the Bay's many coves and inlets. Guided sailing tours are also available, offering a relaxing way to see the area.

- **Fishing**: The Bay is renowned for its fishing. Charter a fishing boat for the day and try your luck catching rockfish, bluefish, or crabs.

- **Kayaking and Paddleboarding**: For a more intimate experience with nature, rent a kayak or paddleboard and explore the Bay's quieter waters. Several outfitters offer guided eco-tours that highlight the region's wildlife and ecosystems.

- **Chesapeake Bay Maritime Museum**: Located in St. Michaels, this museum offers a comprehensive look at the history and culture of the Chesapeake Bay. Exhibits include historic boats, a working boatyard, and interactive displays.

St. Michaels

St. Michaels is a charming waterfront town on Maryland's Eastern Shore, just a short drive from Annapolis. Known for its scenic beauty, historic sites, and maritime heritage, it's a perfect destination for a day trip.

Attractions

- **Chesapeake Bay Maritime Museum**: This expansive museum provides an in-depth look at the maritime history of the Chesapeake Bay. Highlights include the Hooper Strait

Lighthouse, the boatyard, and numerous hands-on exhibits.

- **St. Michaels Winery**: Enjoy a tasting at this local winery, which offers a variety of wines made from grapes grown in Maryland. The relaxed atmosphere and knowledgeable staff make it a pleasant stop for wine enthusiasts.

- **Patriot Cruises**: Take a scenic cruise on the Patriot, a replica of a 1930s steamboat. The narrated tours offer historical insights and beautiful views of the Miles River and Chesapeake Bay.

- **Shops and Restaurants**: St. Michaels is home to a variety of unique shops and excellent restaurants. Stroll along Talbot Street to explore boutiques, art galleries, and eateries offering fresh seafood and local specialties.

Baltimore

Just 30 miles from Annapolis, Baltimore is a vibrant city with a rich history and plenty to see and do. Whether you're interested in museums, sports, or dining, Baltimore has something for everyone.

Attractions

- **Inner Harbor**: The Inner Harbor is the heart of Baltimore and home to several key attractions. Visit the National Aquarium, where you can see thousands of marine creatures, or explore the Maryland Science Center with its interactive exhibits and planetarium.

- **Fort McHenry**: This historic fort is where Francis Scott Key wrote "The Star-Spangled Banner" during the War of 1812. The site offers tours, reenactments, and beautiful views of the harbor.

- **Camden Yards**: Sports fans will enjoy a visit to Oriole Park at Camden Yards, one of the most celebrated ballparks in Major League Baseball. Take a tour of the stadium or catch a Baltimore Orioles game.
- **Fell's Point**: This historic waterfront neighborhood is known for its cobblestone streets, lively pubs, and eclectic shops. It's a great place to enjoy a meal or simply wander and take in the atmosphere.

Washington, D.C.

The nation's capital is just an hour's drive from Annapolis and offers an abundance of iconic landmarks, museums, and cultural experiences. A day trip to Washington, D.C. is a fantastic way to explore some of the country's most important sites.

Attractions

- **National Mall**: The National Mall is home to many of the city's most famous monuments and museums. Visit the Lincoln Memorial, the Washington Monument, and the U.S. Capitol. The Smithsonian Institution's museums, including the National Air and Space Museum and the National Museum of American History, offer free admission and world-class exhibits.

- **The White House**: While tours of the White House require advance planning, the visitor center offers informative exhibits about the history and significance of the President's residence.

- **Georgetown**: This historic neighborhood is known for its charming streets, upscale shops, and waterfront dining. It's a great place to explore on foot and enjoy a meal or coffee.

- **National Zoo**: Part of the Smithsonian Institution, the National Zoo is home to more than 1,500 animals, including the famous giant pandas. Admission is free, making it an excellent family-friendly destination.

Other Nearby Destinations

Beyond the more well-known day trips, there are several other destinations worth exploring near Annapolis.

Annapolis Rock

Located in the South Mountain State Park, Annapolis Rock offers some of the best hiking and scenic views in the region.

- **Hiking**: The hike to Annapolis Rock is about 5 miles round trip and moderately challenging. The trail is well-maintained and offers beautiful views of the forest and valley below.

- **Scenic Views**: At the top, you'll be rewarded with stunning panoramic views of the Appalachian Mountains and Cumberland Valley. It's a great spot for photography, picnicking, or simply enjoying the beauty of nature.

Eastern Shore

The Eastern Shore of Maryland offers a mix of charming towns, beautiful landscapes, and outdoor activities.

- **Oxford**: This small, picturesque town is known for its historic homes, waterfront views, and quiet charm. Take a ride on the Oxford-Bellevue Ferry, the oldest privately operated ferry service in the U.S.

- **Tilghman Island**: This remote island offers a tranquil escape with opportunities for fishing, boating, and exploring local seafood restaurants. The island's relaxed pace and natural beauty make it a perfect day trip destination.

- **Blackwater National Wildlife Refuge**: Located near Cambridge, this refuge is home to a variety of wildlife, including bald eagles, osprey, and migratory waterfowl. The refuge offers hiking trails, scenic drives, and excellent birdwatching opportunities.

Annapolis is ideally located for a variety of day trips and excursions that cater to a wide range of interests. Whether you're exploring the natural beauty of the Chesapeake Bay, enjoying the historic charm of St. Michaels, delving into the vibrant urban life of Baltimore, or experiencing the iconic landmarks of Washington, D.C., there's something for everyone. These destinations provide enriching and memorable experiences that complement your visit to Annapolis, making the region a fantastic hub for exploration and adventure.

Practical Information

When visiting Annapolis, it's essential to be prepared with practical information to ensure a safe and enjoyable trip. Here's a detailed guide covering weather and climate, safety tips, health and medical services, local customs and etiquette, and emergency contacts.

Weather and Climate

Annapolis experiences a humid subtropical climate, characterized by four distinct seasons. Knowing what to expect weather-wise can help you pack appropriately and plan your activities.

Spring (March to May)

- **Temperature**: Average highs range from the mid-50s to the low 70s (Fahrenheit).

- **Weather**: Spring is a pleasant time to visit, with blooming flowers and mild temperatures.

Rain is common, so bringing a rain jacket or umbrella is advisable.

- **What to Pack**: Light layers, a waterproof jacket, and comfortable walking shoes.

Summer (June to August)

- **Temperature**: Average highs are in the mid-80s, occasionally reaching the 90s.

- **Weather**: Summers can be hot and humid, with afternoon thunderstorms. It's the peak tourist season, so expect crowds, especially around the waterfront.

- **What to Pack**: Lightweight clothing, sunscreen, hats, and plenty of water. A light raincoat or umbrella is also useful for sudden showers.

Fall (September to November)

- **Temperature**: Average highs range from the mid-70s in September to the mid-50s by November.

- **Weather**: Fall is a beautiful time to visit, with crisp air and vibrant foliage. Rain is less frequent than in spring.

- **What to Pack**: Layered clothing, as temperatures can vary, and comfortable walking shoes.

Winter (December to February)

- **Temperature**: Average highs are in the mid-40s, with lows dipping into the 30s.

- **Weather**: Winters are generally mild but can be cold, with occasional snowfall. It's a quieter time in Annapolis, with fewer tourists.

- **What to Pack**: Warm clothing, including coats, gloves, and scarves. Waterproof boots are advisable for snowy or rainy days.

Safety Tips

Annapolis is generally a safe city, but it's always wise to take precautions to ensure your safety.

- **Stay Aware**: Be mindful of your surroundings, especially in crowded tourist areas. Keep an eye on your belongings to prevent pickpocketing.

- **Secure Valuables**: Use hotel safes for valuable items like passports, extra cash, and electronics. Avoid carrying large amounts of cash.

- **Night Safety**: Stick to well-lit and populated areas if you're out at night. If possible, travel with a companion.

- **Water Safety**: If you plan to engage in water activities, always wear a life jacket and follow local safety guidelines.

Health and Medical Services

Knowing where to find medical services can be crucial in case of an emergency.

Hospitals and Clinics

- **Anne Arundel Medical Center**: Located at 2001 Medical Parkway, this is the primary hospital in Annapolis, offering comprehensive medical services, including emergency care.

- **Patient First Annapolis**: Located at 2051 West Street, this urgent care center provides walk-in medical services for non-life-threatening conditions.

Pharmacies

- **CVS Pharmacy**: Several locations throughout Annapolis provide prescription medications, over-the-counter drugs, and health-related products.

- **Walgreens**: Another reliable pharmacy chain with multiple locations in the city.

Local Customs and Etiquette

Understanding local customs and etiquette can enhance your experience and help you interact respectfully with residents.

General Etiquette

- **Politeness**: Marylanders are generally polite and friendly. Simple courtesies like saying "please" and "thank you" go a long way.

- **Tipping**: It's customary to tip 15-20% in restaurants. For other services, such as taxis or hairdressers, a tip of 10-15% is appropriate.

- **Queuing**: Always queue in an orderly manner and wait your turn, whether at a bus stop, a store, or a ticket counter.

Specific to Annapolis

- **Nautical Etiquette**: Annapolis has a strong maritime culture. When visiting the harbor or participating in boating activities, respect nautical rules and traditions.

- **Historical Respect**: Annapolis is rich in history. When visiting historical sites, respect the property and any rules or guidelines set by the site.

Emergency Contacts

Having a list of emergency contacts can be incredibly helpful in case of an unexpected situation.

Emergency Services

- **Police, Fire, and Ambulance**: Dial 911 for any emergency situation requiring immediate assistance.

Non-Emergency Contacts

- **Annapolis Police Department**: For non-emergency situations, call (410) 268-9000.

- **Anne Arundel County Fire Department**: For non-emergency situations, call (410) 222-8200.

Medical Assistance

- **Anne Arundel Medical Center**: Emergency Department can be reached at (443) 481-1000.

- **Poison Control Center**: For poison-related emergencies, call 1-800-222-1222.

Local Information

- **Annapolis Visitor Center**: For general information about the city, call (410) 280-0445.

- **Maryland Department of Transportation**: For traffic and travel information, call 1-877-694-8287.

Being well-prepared with practical information can significantly enhance your visit to Annapolis.

Understanding the weather and climate helps you pack appropriately and plan your activities. Following safety tips ensures a secure and enjoyable experience. Knowing where to find health and medical services provides peace of mind, and respecting local customs and etiquette fosters positive interactions. Finally, having emergency contacts at your fingertips ensures you're ready for any unexpected situations. Enjoy your time in Annapolis, knowing you're well-equipped for a smooth and memorable trip.

Resources

When visiting Annapolis, having access to reliable resources can enhance your experience and ensure you make the most of your trip. This section provides a comprehensive list of useful websites, apps, and local contacts that can help you navigate the city, find attractions, and address any needs that may arise during your stay.

Useful Websites and Apps

Official Tourism and City Information

- **Visit Annapolis**: The official tourism website for Annapolis, https://www.visitannapolis.org/ offers a wealth of information on attractions, events, accommodations, dining, and more. It's a great starting point for planning your trip.

- **City of Annapolis**: The official website of the city of Annapolis, https://www.annapolis.gov/

provides information on city services, public transportation, parks, and local government.

- **Historic Annapolis**: For those interested in the city's rich history, https://www.annapolis.org/ offers details on historic sites, museums, tours, and educational programs.

Travel and Navigation

- **Google Maps**: An essential tool for navigation, https://maps.google.com/ provides detailed maps, directions, and real-time traffic updates. It also includes information on nearby restaurants, attractions, and public transit options.

- **Waze**: This community-driven navigation app helps you avoid traffic and find the best routes. https://www.waze.com/ offers real-time updates on road conditions and can be particularly useful for driving around Annapolis.

- **MDTA (Maryland Transportation Authority)**: For information on toll roads, bridges, and tunnels, visit the MDTA website. The site offers updates on traffic conditions and toll rates.

Accommodations and Dining

- **TripAdvisor**: https://www.tripadvisor.com/ is a valuable resource for finding reviews and recommendations for hotels, restaurants, and attractions. The site allows you to read user reviews and compare prices.

- **Yelp**: For dining options, Yelp provides reviews, ratings, and photos of local restaurants, cafes, and bars. It's a great way to discover new places to eat and read about other visitors' experiences.

- **OpenTable**: This app allows you to make reservations at many of Annapolis's restaurants. https://www.opentable.com/ is especially useful for securing a table at popular dining spots.

Attractions and Events

- **Eventbrite**: For finding events, festivals, and activities in Annapolis, https://www.eventbrite.com/ offers a comprehensive listing. You can search by date, type of event, and location.

- **AllTrails**: If you're interested in exploring Annapolis's parks and nature trails, https://www.alltrails.com/ provides detailed maps, trail reviews, and user photos. It's a great app for hikers, bikers, and outdoor enthusiasts.

- **Naval Academy Visitor Center**: The Naval Academy Visitor Center website offers information on tours, events, and visitor policies for the United States Naval Academy.

Local News and Updates

- **The Capital Gazette**: Stay informed about local news and events by visiting the https://www.capitalgazette.com/ Annapolis's primary news source. The website offers news articles, event listings, and community updates.

- **Eye On Annapolis**: This local news website, https://www.eyeonannapolis.net/ provides updates on community events, local news, and dining recommendations.

Local Contacts

Emergency Contacts

- **Police, Fire, and Ambulance**: For any emergency situation requiring immediate assistance, dial 911.

- **Annapolis Police Department**: For non-emergency situations, you can contact the Annapolis Police Department at (410) 268-9000.

- **Anne Arundel County Fire Department**: For non-emergency fire-related issues, call (410) 222-8200.

Medical Services

- **Anne Arundel Medical Center**: Located at 2001 Medical Parkway, the medical center's emergency department can be reached at (443) 481-1000 for any urgent medical needs.

- **Patient First Annapolis**: For non-emergency medical care, visit Patient First at 2051 West Street or call (410) 571-8755.

Transportation

- **Annapolis Transit**: For information on bus routes, schedules, and fares, contact Annapolis Transit at (410) 263-7964 or visit the Annapolis Transit website.

- **SuperShuttle**: For airport transportation services, SuperShuttle can be reached at (800)

258-3826 or through their https://www.supershuttle.com/

- **Yellow Cab of Annapolis**: For taxi services, contact Yellow Cab at (410) 268-1212.

Tourism and Visitor Information

- **Annapolis Visitor Center**: For general information about the city, maps, and brochures, visit the Annapolis Visitor Center at 26 West Street or call (410) 280-0445.

- **Chesapeake Bay Maritime Museum**: For information on exhibits, events, and tours, contact the museum at (410) 745-2916 or visit their https://www.cbmm.org/.

Local Utilities and Services

- **BGE (Baltimore Gas and Electric)**: For utility services, including electricity and gas, contact BGE at (800) 685-0123 or visit their https://www.bge.com/

- **Annapolis Public Works**: For city services such as water, sewer, and waste management, contact the Department of Public Works at (410) 263-7949 or visit the city's website.

Having access to these useful websites, apps, and local contacts can greatly enhance your visit to Annapolis. Whether you need information on accommodations, dining, attractions, or emergency services, these resources provide comprehensive support to ensure a smooth and enjoyable trip. Make the most of your time in Annapolis by leveraging these tools to navigate the city, stay informed, and discover all that this charming destination has to offer.

Conclusion

As you close this Annapolis Travel Guide 2024, we hope you feel inspired and well-prepared to embark on your journey to this captivating city. Annapolis, with its rich history, vibrant culture, and scenic beauty, offers an unforgettable experience for every visitor. Whether you're exploring the historic landmarks, sailing the Chesapeake Bay, savoring local cuisine, or simply strolling through the charming streets, Annapolis promises to enchant and delight.

A City Steeped in History

Annapolis's historical significance is evident at every turn. As the capital of Maryland and a pivotal city in American history, it offers a deep dive into the past. Walking tours of the historic district, visits to the United States Naval Academy, and tours of the Maryland State House provide fascinating insights into the city's colonial and revolutionary heritage. Each historic site tells a story, contributing to the rich tapestry that makes Annapolis so unique.

Vibrant Cultural Experiences

The cultural scene in Annapolis is as diverse as it is vibrant. The city's numerous galleries, theaters, and museums celebrate a wide range of artistic expressions and historical narratives. Annual events and festivals, such as the Annapolis Film Festival and the First Sunday Arts Festival, highlight the city's commitment to fostering a lively arts community. These cultural experiences are a testament to Annapolis's dynamic spirit and its residents' dedication to preserving and promoting the arts.

Outdoor Adventures

For those who love the outdoors, Annapolis is a paradise. The Chesapeake Bay offers endless opportunities for sailing, boating, kayaking, and fishing. The city's parks and nature trails provide beautiful settings for hiking, biking, and picnicking. Whether you're an avid sailor or a casual nature enthusiast, the natural beauty of Annapolis is sure to captivate you.

Culinary Delights

Annapolis's culinary scene is a delightful reflection of its coastal heritage and diverse culture. From fine dining restaurants to casual seafood shacks, the city offers a wide array of dining options. Savoring Maryland blue crabs, fresh oysters, and other local specialties is a must for any visitor. The city's craft breweries, wineries, and coffee shops add to the vibrant food and drink landscape, ensuring there's something for every palate.

Family-Friendly Activities

Families visiting Annapolis will find a wealth of activities that cater to all ages. Kid-friendly attractions like the Annapolis Maritime Museum,

Pirate Adventures on the Chesapeake, and the Chesapeake Children's Museum provide educational and entertaining experiences. Parks, playgrounds, and family-oriented events ensure that there's always something fun to do with the kids.

Day Trips and Excursions

Annapolis's convenient location makes it an excellent base for exploring nearby destinations. Day trips to the charming town of St. Michaels, the bustling city of Baltimore, or the nation's capital, Washington, D.C., offer diverse experiences just a short drive away. Whether you're seeking additional history, cultural experiences, or outdoor adventures, the surrounding region provides endless possibilities.

Practical Information

Being well-prepared with practical information can significantly enhance your visit.

Understanding the local weather, safety tips, health and medical services, and local customs ensures a smooth and enjoyable trip. Having access to emergency contacts and useful resources, such as websites and apps, provides peace of mind and helps you navigate the city with ease.

A Warm Welcome

The warmth and hospitality of Annapolis's residents are integral to the city's charm. Visitors are welcomed with open arms and treated to genuine friendliness and helpfulness. Whether you're chatting with a local shop owner, dining at a family-run restaurant, or exploring the city's historic sites, the people of Annapolis make every moment special.

In Closing

Annapolis is a city that effortlessly blends the past with the present, offering a unique and enriching experience for every visitor. As you plan your trip, let this guide serve as a valuable resource, helping you to discover all that Annapolis has to offer. From its historic landmarks and cultural treasures to its natural beauty and culinary delights, Annapolis is a destination that will leave you with lasting memories and a longing to return.

We hope your visit to Annapolis is filled with adventure, discovery, and joy. Enjoy every moment of your journey in this remarkable city. Safe travels and happy exploring!

Frequently Asked Questions (FAQs)

1. When is the best time to visit Annapolis?

The best time to visit Annapolis depends on your interests:

- **Spring (March to May)**: Mild temperatures and blooming flowers make this a great time for outdoor activities and exploring the city.

- **Summer (June to August)**: Warm weather and a bustling waterfront, perfect for boating and enjoying outdoor festivals. However, it can be crowded.

- **Fall (September to November)**: Cooler temperatures and beautiful fall foliage. This is a great time for walking tours and attending local events.

- **Winter (December to February)**: Quieter and colder, but the city's holiday decorations and events, like the Annapolis Chocolate Binge Festival, add a festive atmosphere.

2. How do I get to Annapolis?

Annapolis is accessible by various means of transportation:

- **By Air**: The nearest major airport is Baltimore/Washington International Thurgood Marshall Airport (BWI), about 25 miles away. Washington Dulles International Airport (IAD) and Ronald Reagan Washington National Airport (DCA) are also nearby.

- **By Car**: Annapolis is easily accessible via major highways such as US Route 50/301.

- **By Train**: While Annapolis doesn't have a train station, Amtrak services BWI Airport and New Carrollton, with transfers to local transportation.

- **By Bus**: Several bus services, including Greyhound and Megabus, connect Annapolis with nearby cities.

3. What are the must-see attractions in Annapolis?

- **United States Naval Academy**: Offers guided tours and showcases naval history.

- **Maryland State House**: The oldest state capitol in continuous legislative use, with historical exhibits.

- **Historic Downtown Annapolis**: Features colonial architecture, shops, and restaurants.

- **William Paca House and Garden**: A restored 18th-century mansion and garden.

- **Banneker-Douglass Museum**: Highlights African American history in Maryland.

- **Annapolis Maritime Museum**: Focuses on the maritime heritage of the Chesapeake Bay.

4. Where can I find good places to eat in Annapolis?

Annapolis offers a wide range of dining options:

- **Fine Dining**: Try Reynolds Tavern, Carrol's Creek Café, or Lewnes' Steakhouse.

- **Casual Dining**: Boatyard Bar & Grill, Miss Shirley's Café, and Federal House Bar & Grille are popular choices.

- **Local Cuisine**: Don't miss Maryland blue crabs, crab cakes, and fresh oysters at places like Cantler's Riverside Inn and The Choptank.

5. What family-friendly activities are available in Annapolis?

- **Annapolis Maritime Museum & Park**: Interactive exhibits and summer camps.

- **Pirate Adventures on the Chesapeake**: Pirate-themed cruises for kids.

- **Chesapeake Children's Museum**: Hands-on exhibits and educational programs.

- **Parks and Playgrounds**: Quiet Waters Park, Truxtun Park, and Jonas Green Park offer outdoor fun and activities.

6. Are there any good shopping areas in Annapolis?

- **Historic Downtown Shops**: Unique boutiques, antique stores, and specialty shops on Main Street and Maryland Avenue.

- **Artisanal Markets**: The Annapolis Market House and the Annapolis Farmers Market offer local crafts, produce, and specialty foods.

- **Malls and Boutiques**: Westfield Annapolis Mall and Annapolis Towne Centre offer a mix of retail stores and dining options.

7. What outdoor activities can I enjoy in Annapolis?

- **Sailing and Boating**: Rent a sailboat, take a sailing course, or join a guided boat tour.

- **Parks and Nature Trails**: Explore Quiet Waters Park, Sandy Point State Park, and Greenbury Point Nature Center.

- **Water Sports**: Kayaking, paddleboarding, and fishing are popular activities.

- **Golf**: Play a round at The Golf Club at South River, Annapolis Golf Club, or Eisenhower Golf Course.

8. What are some good day trips from Annapolis?

- **Chesapeake Bay**: Boating, fishing, and exploring the Bay's natural beauty.

- **St. Michaels**: Charming waterfront town with the Chesapeake Bay Maritime Museum and scenic cruises.

- **Baltimore**: Visit the Inner Harbor, National Aquarium, and Fort McHenry.

- **Washington, D.C.**: Explore the National Mall, Smithsonian museums, and historic landmarks.

9. **What practical information should I know before visiting Annapolis?**

- **Weather and Climate**: Annapolis has four distinct seasons, with hot summers and mild winters. Pack accordingly.

- **Safety Tips**: Stay aware of your surroundings, secure valuables, and follow water safety guidelines.

- **Health and Medical Services**: Anne Arundel Medical Center and Patient First Annapolis provide medical care.

- **Local Customs and Etiquette**: Marylanders are polite and friendly. Tipping is customary in restaurants and for services.

10. What resources are available for more information?

- **Visit Annapolis**: Official tourism website with comprehensive information.

- **Google Maps and Waze**: Essential for navigation and real-time traffic updates.

- **TripAdvisor and Yelp**: For reviews and recommendations on hotels, restaurants, and attractions.

- **Annapolis Visitor Center**: Offers maps, brochures, and general information about the city.

We hope these FAQs help you plan a smooth and enjoyable visit to Annapolis. Enjoy your trip and make the most of everything this historic and vibrant city has to offer!